Ounces of Oneness

Nejoud Al-Yagout

Unmasked

What stays is unknown
as we undress each other
of labels

A millisecond is more
than enough to remind
us that love is naked

This is liberation from
veils, clouds and
ammunition

Awe-struck

Scattered bullets, scraped knees on
side-streets of devotion, a heart
bleeding in overdrive, tears for
an ounce of oneness

Nobody can quite explain it,
but we choose to go to hell for one
another to find our paradise
on the way to:

this

This

This is the feeling that shifts paradigms,
slowly coming close to the poignant glory
and stillness of moonless nights
where the look on the face of a child is priceless,
for he managed to stay up past nine

And love can make it as surreal as a dragonfly chewing
what remains of a butterfly on a sidewalk of dreams

And this is the touch that grazes shoulders,
where chemicals are so intense that adrenalin
becomes a thing of the past

This *whatever-it-is* will be remembered for eons
for it managed to reach the desperation beneath
rib cages, the *aah* in tonsils, the *oof* in sighs,
heaving closely beneath the surface of a smile

And this is all a mathematical equation,
so something inside whispers loudly to you
that this is exactly how it ought to be
and it ought to be grand just like *this*,
just like in a moment where the panic is so intense
you feel hounded and thoughts of bodies strewn
on a deserted beach take you into a daydream, resurrected,
to stop the inner voice from raping you, again and again
mercilessly

So you think deeply of having your thoughts caressed,
your essence pulled into a vortex of forgetfulness
as waves of surrender pulsate in your veins

In this, you regain composure though madness
grips your hand forcefully, provoking your sanity
with a fire iron, burning all that you thought was you

And you rise, a phoenix from the ashes
surrounded by *this*, touched by the intangibility
of *this*, *this*, this nameless force that pushes you
to the brink of sin taking you to the embers of hell
dragging you to Paradise back and forth, back and forth
as you whirl in a state of emergency emerging, merging
and in your metamorphosis you sing:

> *I am the gazelle, and the lion is ravaging me,*
> *though I am wide awake, still alive*
> *This does not lessen the pain,*
> *but it reminds me of terrorists*
> *Somehow I think of them a lot these days,*
> *which is why I stopped watching the news,*
> *because feeling vulnerable in a mall sucks,*
> *and it is in this constant replay of shards of glass*
> *and bloodstained spectacles* on *a black and white*
> *marble floor that I remember you*

Yes. I think of terrorists, but not quite as much
as I think of you, dammit,
which brings me now to this feeling, exacerbated,
for the pain is haunting me beneath my veins,
beneath the folds of skin and the chest bones
that are too protruding for an adult scanner probe

'Next time we have to use the children's one on you,'
she said, forgetting to add that there will not be a
next time hopefully, as she pushed and shoved,
trying to see what was wrong with me

People tend to forget when to hope, although they
are hoping all the time, in every encounter,
with every paycheck, each message received,
looks that say yes,
way before screaming yes, yes, oh yes!

And so I watch my flesh pulsating in the
mouth of the lion
and I fall in love with Life's take, give
And this is why, surely this is why, the poet must live

Ever-awake

Through verse, untruths are weaved
into the multi-colored fabrics of our psyche

The life-force penetrates polarities;
projects dualities; embodies the
I Am, the Om, the Hu

Awake in the game of pretending,
ever-awake in the eternity of a scream

Conditioning

Shouting,
shaking the sweat
out of pores,
tossing, turning,
etching hearts on
dilapidated desks

But there you were
And that's all it took
for something,
for anything
to give

Black Hole

Everything and nothing,
I say, when they ask
what I follow
and in *I-don't-know*,
I find you

Life dances in the vein,
not in the vain

A Cup of the Beyond

In humility,
we tiptoe around
I-told-you-so,
still in recovery
from the way
we were loved

The path is for
everybody, not
nobody

This memory lurks
in our DNA, and we
ask to be inebriated

Divine

Be my wine
Intoxicate me

Oh for a sip of
you, me and the void
where we know not
the concept of we

Be my wine so I can stay
silent in the space
where there is no
yours, mine

In this *pane-et-circenses* realm,
you are my *pane*
you are my *circenses*

Semper Fi

An empire built on
clipped wings

Order brought
disorder to the mind

We learned - once upon
a yesteryear - that the heart
is the only place where
nobody dies

Ascension

Immortal love,
ablaze

We can only fix
what is broken,
I assured myself,
as I picked up what
remained of me,
and not much remained,
until consciousness
reinvented itself

Upping the Ante

Alas!

Once the water-bound fish
has seen the shore and
the sky and the beyond,
possibility beckons

First, to defy gravity,
to reprogram every cell
in the physical body
in the energetic field
to give up the gills, fins, scales,
even the water known as home

This is the price paid for
awareness

Evolution

Who are you?

Are you?

You?

Perplexed

and the questions arise, over and over

we lay here contemplating the sky spreading its
tentacles, a blushing petal, whirling dervishes of
crescendos, the tender salsa of gravity that pulls us
constantly toward

you,
the nameless

Shedding

Your name, assigned

We cannot ascend this way
We cannot transcend this way

In mind-chatter, there are lines, institutions,
various colors - apart from those of the rainbow -
when all I want is to embrace all

Universality

Allow me the honor to love those you hate,
to include those who you exclude

Allow me the honor to make peace with those
upon whom you declare war and allow me to
befriend your enemies

Let me kiss those from other sects, faiths
and make love to the wayward, the wizards,
the astray, the clowns and so-called fools

I didn't come all the way to earth
to love only you

I didn't come all the way to earth
to love only me

Connection

Falling in love with all, heaven awakens
inside of us, elephants rejoice, the dew of surrender
is sprinkled on gardens of now, and crying and laughing
are the same,

says the guide
inside

Inner Guru

this voice is louder
than any other
though it does
not speak

Self-inquiry

Voicelessly,
even perception is
perceived

deeper,

deeper

and as the path gets
steeper
steeper

you
rise
above

superficiality

Sight

The surface, illusory

There is only what one knows,
and knowing is the stellar waltz of
realization

A-ha!

In belief, I gave up knowledge
In knowledge, I gave up belief
Finally, I gave up both
only to find you t(here) chanting:

> *You come here to rid yourself of fear*
> *only to cling to your attachments*
> *but only in your detachment*
> *can the beloved come near*
>
> *To free yourself from pain,*
> *you need not completely die*
> *but by merging the i with I*
> *the self will remain*

No Notions

Self-awareness: serenity in the eye of
the hurricane, silence beneath thoughts
deemed insane, tranquility beyond judgment
and pain

Self-awareness: stillness in a heartbeat
that manifests again and again
ad infinitum.

Listening

On an on,
we hear
the drumbeats of
deathlessness

And in mango groves,
dancing beneath a still crescent,
two become one

Uno

Only those far away
are deluded by this
phenomenon known as
duality

Only those who close
their inner eye are veiled
from reality

Dual-duel

I slay countless dragons
and walk the tightrope
of confusion,

resigned to the fact
that I can only realize
myself through you

Are we one or two?
Are we one or two?

As old becomes new,
the seeker arises
and bliss appears

Where?

Right Here

In the gap between breaths

I sit still, losing a self
I never was

Is it ST depression or an awakening?

The crickets fall asleep and the rain stops
pounding on my electric aura as I ask:

What gift are you bringing to me?
What is it that I refuse to see?

Pain eases up and replies:

Finally...

And the journey begins
into the desert of me

Dunes

I wash my face in a mirage,
                    becoming water

I do not care or perhaps I care
                    too much

about sandstorms,
cacti, falcons
and all that jazz,
                    but I know so well:

                    We are dunes.
And I can finally breathe

Adieu

In circles of inhales,
exhales, identity ceases

I count the cracks on the wall
and slam a crystal door, shattering
an illusory façade, finding solace in
cobble-stoned roads and electric-blue
cornfields as eagles hover above me

Awakening pushes, pulls,
you push, pull
and I begin another search

Oh My!

I look everywhere, when all I see
are purple hearts and crocodile tears,
scrambling around city walls

Something resonates until absence
becomes presence

Suddenly,
I know nothing

Grammatica

I dove into *scio nescio* and
rented a *Colombina*,
when all I wanted was a place to
hide from them, from me,
from you

And though you were a comma,
you felt like a full-stop.

Still we dash -
and dash -
into each other

It will take the illusion of time to
register that
we are one - unveiled -
in one, of one

Era by era,
a new theory

Another Hypothesis

And so you called with an epiphany:
Perhaps we are all computer simulations

Though you sounded elated,
I met you in your sadness

    as we tangoed
        again
    and
        again

into the unknown,
preparing for the battle

Facing

Warriors stumbling at the frontline
Feelings - ambassadors of the ego -
drag us back into the mud
of worldly ways

Resonation reverberates,
and oh what a frisson of delight –
that glorious moment when we finally
acknowledge that doubting doubt
is heresy, pure blasphemy at its best

Sapience

Unsure, raging

Phantoms
in a reverie
swim in
a ball of fire
at redneck speed,
contemplating

Peripatos

Could it be an opening into myself, into you,
into the world that appears, disappears?

Could it be singular, plural, infinite?

Could it be the space before goodbye or
the tune of glistening palm trees swaying to thunder?

Perhaps it is a lighthouse portal?

I sigh
and read your instructions

Anything for Peace

You tell me to lie down on a hard surface
and lose myself in bones, flesh

The collective sees diamond antlers on a deer
sprawling lime-green hills nail-biting queens
hiding beneath mirrored multi-patched quilts
crystal balls magic jelly-capsules ice-cold
waiting rooms cringe-worthy declarations of love
pots of lemongrass tea

The collective sees you, me
and a perceived enemy

We hold each other
and place flowers in our being
and vultures in our essence

There are no enemies,
the only enemy is belief

Oh! I have so much to say,
so much to ask
before you push the button

Ode To A Terrorist

You are a thought, manifested
Whose thought are you? Yours, mine, ours?

Somewhere beyond the temporal, spatial
we were one

Read your heart: there are sonnets of love,
yet you make it so complicated
believing thoughts that are not even yours
dancing to others' projections
basking in the madness of the collective

Awaken! Some of you have…
In this world of polarities,
is there a me, a you?

Meet me on the moon
Let's drink stardust and talk of our demons

I hate this hate I have toward you
I hate this hate you have toward me
I hate this hate, I hate this hate
Let's surrender

Fear and love cannot grasp each other

Isn’t That So!

they may make love - star-crossed lovers - but they
won't hold hands under a veil of stars while dancing
around a fire strumming ukuleles made with passion
and dreams

they won't hold hands

because, just because

Transition

And so they are untouchables
to one another,
that is the unspoken treaty

The fire of desire is extinguished
with the pretense of indifference -
though all are yearned for *secretly*

Life-life

Oh for a piece of him and her to remind us
that there is only eternity, that transience
is a delusion of grandeur while we sway to
paradoxes and fill the void with
everything

Transcendence

From a hole to whole

The body reveals
what the heart conceals

I will hide
I will hide my darkness
if you run away
from your own

I won't say no to us
but I'll never use a prayer to
ask for you

I love you too much to turn you
into a wish that was granted to
me against your will

Instead, I give you the freedom
to live, to love without me

But I'll never say no to us

Implications

I nod my head
to the rhythm of yes
and melt into my beloved

All are of the beloved

And we fall in love
Once is never enough

Non-resistance

We succumb again and again

It's primordial,
written, and this
is nothing new

They say it is
a turbulent ride on
waves of chaos

But what I have
with you
is a dance in a ballroom

Ours

Oh as we waltz in the eye of the
hurricane and shuffle with the storm,
slaughtered; oh as the prodding rivers of lust
dance in our veins, pulling us where we so want to go:
into the bed of yes and no

All this for an epiphany, for in case you haven't noticed,
we are slowly becoming everything
to one another, and in this *I-don't-know* t
hat we have painted on Love's canvas,
we remain handcuffed to the rest of them

There is more in us - we know it -
and when we succumb, so does our fear,
and as we hang our minds with the clothes to dry,
we recall the warning
when we dove back once into the unknown

This is not just an elephant in the room
It's the universe, it's our universe, somehow

And it was unbearable when we walked alone,
even if for a while, for we had become intimately
acquainted with our idea, a fetus of love, and red was finally
splashed on whitewashed walls, red and purple too,
that's the way we liked it, *like* it, beneath all the layers

We contemplate how they can call this evil,
this seed that led to us

All we had to do is choose and choice overtook us

You see, lovers, ours is neither for gazelles nor swans,
and after this has registered, it will be exactly like
that moment when a war is over, that timeless moment
when you can actually feel the void between
a flower and its roots

And in case we have blocked out the rays of the sun,
we are reminded that learning how to love
is a star bursting in the galaxy, it happens all the time

We may romanticize it, but it is actually filled with a
fiery push and shove that lies and calls itself love

Still, we found each other among the violent particles
exploding into existence, clamoring to occupy space,
until there was no other way but to us

What is ours is a twist, a blow to having, knowing

We have no immunity to what is so recklessly,
deliciously ours, and that's what makes it
so explosive

Big-Banging

In that momentary eruption
of consciousness,
the yearning began for this,
that and

you,
my last
rung
on the
ladder
of me

You always knew that I
would cut myself,
willingly,
with the razor that is you

Touch

Bleeding on the edges of one another,
we are so close that I touch your
struggle, your joie de vivre and the energy of
others who gaze intently as I cartwheel
in the corridors of your come and go

This touch is the universe belting out an aria,
strumming the strings of a vintage violin

I touch your intangibility only to find
that I am touching the deepest part of me

The Cliff

In profundity,
we teeter on the edges
of wanting, knowing,
accepting that
we cannot be this way
without ruffling the feathers
of conditioned thoughts

In other words:
If you can't love, please leave
If you can't leave, please love

In Love's Constitution

The conditions of love
prod you gently to the forest
where berries plead to stain
your lips, your tongue

In love's constitution, there are wolves
trapped in vortices of repression

In love's constitution, parallelism
stifles the flow as you become intimate
with beginnings and endings,
endings and beginnings

The Dance

Life
is
the
formless
manifesting
as
form;
Death
is
the
form
returning
to
formlessness

Multiverses

And we rest in the middle
of two worlds, sowing the
seeds of letting go

For when attached to the song
of a bird, the roar of the lion
will faze you

Until you reach
the point where awe is
ever-present
but nothing can amaze you

Orb

You are no longer surprised at
the melody of nonresistance,
and as leaves fall, you can almost hear
acceptance

Nature knows not the word no

And this is why the brooks
bleed in our core and you quietly
whisper to the world, prior to surrender:

I want to be tired of you
because at least that way
I had you somehow

The Collapse

Resting, finally,
on the wings of ascension,
love asks not:

Who?
What?
Where?
When?
Why?

To the seeker and the sought,
it gently whispers:

Befriend the other,
you are the other

99%

You think you can touch me
in places, unseen,
but I am here to tell you
that you are me, and in this dance of
non-duality, there is no we

The greatest love story ever told was
between a leaf and the sun,
between the trees and a breeze,
between the sand beneath your feet
and the ocean,
between you and me

And in this oneness that
transcends all,
the stars remind us
that we are 99% space,
and the 1% really does not matter

www.ingramcontent.com/pod-product-compliance
Lightning Source LLC
LaVergne TN
LVHW091237150826
845673LV00003B/1184

* 9 7 8 1 5 4 8 7 3 2 7 0 7 *